MENTOR WONDERS

Copyright © 2022 by Catherine Lee

All rights reserved. No part of this book may be reproduced in any manner whatsoever without written permission except in the case of brief quotations embodied in critical articles and reviews.

First Printing, 2023
by Cheshire Cat Composition

This creative writing project was funded in part by
a 2022 Individual Artist grant by the City of San Antonio,
Department of Arts & Culture.

PRINT ISBN 978-0-9833483-1-3
0-9833483-1-6

E-BOOK ISBN 978-0-9833483-2-0

MENTOR WONDERS

A One Act Play

Revised Edition

CATHERINE LEE

Cheshire Cat Composition

*This writing project is the culmination
of a lifetime's worth of personal mentoring
by educators Frank Marbach and Percy E. Johnston;
writer tedjoans; multimedia artists James Sanders and
David Cort;
and dramatic actor/directors,
Tony Plana, Carlos Lacamara and,
most especially,
Bill Gundry*

CONTENTS

Dedication — iv
Development Notes — vii
Cast of Characters — ix
The Setting, The Time — xi
Author's Notes — xiii
Foreword — xv

1
DRAMATIC SCRIPT — 1

Scene 1 — 2

Locked, Loaded, Dreadfully Drilled — 6

Scene 2 — 10

If Walls Could Talk — 15

Scene 3 — 18

Alien Bunny — 25

Scene 4 — 27

Hippo Face Off — 29

Scene 5	36
Missing Piece (For Jason)	44

2
INTRODUCTION TO THE POEMS — 47

Age Difference	49
Messy Business	50
Laces Rule	52
Cake Mix Stories	54
Cobalt: Keeping What Passed Present	57
'Rithmetic: Fractions, Mysteries, Curiosities	59
Like Dominos	61
Crescendo	64
When This Mentor Gets Puzzled	66
Keeping Score	67
Acknowledgments	70
Stage With Cafeteria	73
Stage With Mentor Room	74
About The Author	80

DEVELOPMENT NOTES

Mentor Wonders was developed between January-October 2022 during a series of Zoom-recorded rehearsals by actors from San Antonio's theater community including members of the Seniors In Play Readers' Theater. The project was funded in part by a grant from the City of San Antonio, Department of Arts & Culture.

Final script dress rehearsal segments were directed by Angela Otey, recorded between August-October 2022 and assembled into a Dramatic Reading video. Backgrounds selection, costume consultation, and video storyboard creation by Catherine Lee. Original music composed by Cecil Reenald Carter. Video post-production by James E Sanders Jr. The *Mentor Wonders* Dramatic Reading video premiered on Nov. 18, 2022 at Woodlawn Pointe, San Antonio, Texas, and was subsequently released online. The cast, in order of appearance, consisted of:

> Terry Lake ..... Adele Herzstein
> Carlos Castillo ..... Eduardo C. Garza
> Jason Peterson ..... Robert M. Moritz
> Sandra Kenney ..... Angela Otey
> Barbara Minton ..... H. B. Robinson
> Linda Hale ..... Mildred Hilbricht
> Joey Green ..... Rosemary Livar
> Pearl Houston, Ph.D. ..... Mary Williams

CAST OF CHARACTERS

IN ORDER OF APPEARANCE

TERRY LAKE, staff Community Coordinator at Confianza Academy, manages program, assigns mentors, and schedules group events.

CARLOS CASTILLO, veteran mentor, one of the few bilingual mentors, works at a research institute. He was paired with Tomas Fuentes beginning last year. Their close male-centric bond helped Tomas compensate for his papa's absence.

JASON PETERSON, prospective mentoring volunteer, is an architect at a large firm. Detail-oriented to a fault, he interrupts with difficult questions, to compare this program to others he's considering.

POETA TAMBIÉN (optional cast) is a bilingual Spanish reader of "Dreamscape" poems with music background as daydreams that interrupt meeting dialog. If only one poet is cast, this character has priority.

SANDRA KENNEY is a retired educator of special needs children who has been mentoring since the program started nine years ago. She helps coordinate and recruit mentors.

BARBARA MINTON, veteran mentor, works in book publishing. She mentored Angela several years ago for the *Alien Bunny* creative project.

CAST OF CHARACTERS

LINDA HALE, veteran mentor, also bilingual in Spanish, is a retired school nurse who has mentored Beryl Fuentes for three years. She helps Beryl deal with family instability caused by her mother's severe illness.

JOEY GREEN is younger, a prospective new mentor. An ophthalmologic technician, this character can be either male or female.

PEARL HOUSTON, Ph.D. has been Principal at Confianza Academy for the past five years. She instituted incentives to improve attendance and graduation rates, including mentoring, to counter her school's poor test-score performance.

POET DREAMER (optional cast) also recites poems with music background as daydreams that interrupt meeting dialog, alternating these "Dreamscapes" with Poeta También.

ANGELA FERNANDEZ (optional cast) is a student mentee, one of the co-authors who reads her *Alien Bunny* story to the Mentor Coordinator and Principal, either live on stage or as a video projection.

PHONE VOICE is an AMBER Alert automated announcement that comes through on all phones.

TOMAS FUENTES (optional cast) is a bilingual student mentee, Beryl's older brother, paired with Carlos. Family issues cause his papa to abduct him and move to Mexico. He reads a letter he's written to Carlos, either live on stage or as a video projection.

THE SETTING, THE TIME

THE SETTING
The first four scenes take place during an Orientation for new and returning volunteer mentors at Confianza Academy, a bilingual public school in San Antonio, Texas. This gathering takes place in the school's Cafeteria, where the group is clustered around two tables, with school staff at the front. The fifth scene, several months later, takes place in the school's dedicated Mentor Room, and during a phone call between the Mentor Coordinator and a veteran mentor at his workplace.

THE TIME
A new school year in the fall of 2016, early September and mid-November. It's been some years since a heavily-armed attacker invaded Sandy Hook Elementary School in Newtowne, Connecticut. But another more recent armed ambush of Dallas, Texas police has some volunteers concerned about school safety.

AUTHOR'S NOTES

"Dreamscapes," music video-like interruptions containing poetry and illustrations, occasionally appear. These can be staged either as complete videos projected on scrim, or directed to one or two additional actors, Poet Dreamer and Poeta También. Should actors perform these parts, they stand on one of four elevated platform stage areas obscured by scrim, arranged in an inverted V shape, two to a side behind the main stage (see diagrams at end of script). Projections of various scenes in motion or as stills appear on darkened scrim where indicated.

Also treated dramatically like Dreamscapes are the readings by two former mentees. One, Angela Fernandez, reads her story, "Alien Bunny," to school officials. A second, Tomas Fuentes, writes a letter of appreciation to his former mentor. These stories can either appear as video projections on scrim, or be portrayed by actors reading from elevated platforms at the rear of the main stage.

FOREWORD

It is a distinct pleasure to introduce the work of writer and poet Catherine Lee. We first met in early 2018 through a theatrical program called Seniors in Play that I founded with the late iconic San Antonio actor/director Bill Gundry, in which seniors tell the myriad stories acquired from long lives rich with experiences.

Cat, as she prefers to be called, already dedicated to writing and reciting poetry, embraced this process wholeheartedly. In her own words, "My personal goal has been to improve skills when reading original poetry, both with musicians and as monologues." Through Seniors in Play she accomplished that and much more.

Mentor Wonders is an autobiographical dramatization performed by Seniors in Play actors based on her own experience as a school mentor. It is a fascinating hybrid of form and content, utilizing several art genres to capture the different dimensions of a lived social service: in the context of a standard documentary enactment, Cat allows the viewer to understand empathically the challenges and rewards of her multifaceted experience.

Throughout this process I have witnessed Cat's identity transform with an expanded sense of self and of community. Constantly processing experience and expressing it meaningfully she has become a prolific creator of expressive art resulting in deepening connections with herself, her fellow artists, her family, and her friends. She is an inspiring example of how the arts can revitalize and fulfill.

Enjoy her latest collaboration and prepare yourself for the next. While you are reading this brief introduction and her play, Cat will certainly be working on her next project.

Tony Plana
Seniors in Play

1

Dramatic Script

Scene 1

Mentor Orientation in Cafeteria begins with welcome speeches and discussion.

The lights go up on the front of the Cafeteria at Confianza Academy on a school day morning. Two long tables are set up. Terry Lake, staff Community Coordinator, enters carrying a stack of handouts, to lead a Mentor Orientation meeting. On one table, she puts the pile of handouts. Several veterans and prospective mentors wander in and take seats at tables, either in friend groupings or as individuals. Terry goes to the front of the room, which is staged diagonally stage right, relative to the tables. She has no lectern or mic.

Greetings are heard around the room before Terry starts speaking. Terry gestures to those arriving.

TERRY: Morning, folks. Come on in. We're just getting started.

When Terry begins addressing them, greetings subside.

TERRY: Welcome everybody to Confianza Academy. It's wonderful to see all of you, new volunteers and veteran mentors alike. I'm Terry Lake. I'm the school's Community Coordinator, your contact person with your mentees. I'll match you with a student, based on your interests and their needs. I'll be giving you a Mentor Handbook and two forms in a second.

Carlos Castillo, a veteran mentor, jumps up from his seat and picks up the pile of handouts.

CARLOS: I'll help you pass those out, Terry.

TERRY: Thanks Carlos. Glad to see you're back. Tomas told me he can't wait to see you again.

Carlos passes a packet to each mentor while Terry speaks.

TERRY: New folks, mentoring is usually scheduled back-to-back from 9 A.M. 'til 2 P.M. You normally spend that hour in our mentoring room which is adjacent to my office. I've stocked it with craft supplies, books, and all sorts of games.

From here on, throughout the play, projections of still and motion video interactions between mentors and mentees appear randomly on one to four scrims behind the actors on stage. These continue during school staff dialog, stopping when scrim lighting allows reveal of a platform stage where a poet or mentee performs.

The first time you meet your mentee, you might ask them to show you around the school or visit the library. You and your mentee decide together how to structure each one-hour weekly visit. This helps them develop analytic and decision-making skills. Mentoring touches a child in a way that helps emotionally too. Making that connection is gratifying because you can see the child's growth. Maybe not the first week, or the second. Give it a month or two, isn't that so, veterans? After that, if it's really not working, I'll find a different mentee for you.

In that packet, please find the background check permission form. New volunteers need to sign and return that form today. Returning mentors have already done theirs. All school personnel, including volunteers, are required to pass a background check. Don't worry. We don't count minor offenses like traffic tickets. But we must exclude anyone known to be a threat to students. If you have any concerns, please see me after the meeting.

New mentor volunteer Jason Peterson interrupts Terry with a concern.

JASON: Before I commit to coming here to volunteer, I'd like to know more about security. Does this school have plans for what to do if a serious situation develops?

TERRY: Excellent question. To get into the building for this meeting, you've all just gone through our visitors' protocol of locked doors, buzzed admittance, sign in with ID, and wear badges. But if you mean drills, we do have both Tornado and Fire Drills. During those drills, you would go with your mentee, who has been taught where to shelter and wait.

If you mean — god forbid — an "active shooter" situation, again, yes. We do have a school-wide drill protocol involving locked doors, covered windows, and hiding. We do not promote fighting back against armed intruders, if that's what concerns you. Please, read about our lockdown drill ahead of time in the Handbook. After you all start actively mentoring, we will schedule another meeting to explain it and practice as a group. An actual drill might happen while you're here. It would be a total surprise, unannounced, coordinated with police. Unfortunately, nobody can be warned that it's only a drill. That makes it extremely stressful.

Terry's speech is interrupted by the Dreamscape, "Locked, Loaded, Dreadfully Drilled." Poeta También appears on an elevated platform behind the scrim located at center left behind the main stage. She performs the poem while images of school shooters and lockdown drills are projected on the other three darkened scrims. The Orientation attendees mime continuing to meet during the Dreamscape.

Locked, Loaded, Dreadfully Drilled

*Our fire drills in elementary school
were almost festive.
We filed as classes,
grouped in orderly lines,
to designated places on a playground.
We kids considered these events were
extra recess opportunities,
welcome interruptions to a boring day.
These modern days of heightened threats
have transfigured thrill to anguish.
When practicing to stay alive
in face of random lethal bullets
from omnipresent firearms,
we cannot know if armed attack
this day is drill or real.*

*Silence is essential
during active shooter episodes.
Be an absolutely quiet target*

*in darkened room, hopefully invisible
behind drawn window blinds, blocked door.
In huddled corners, waiting for whatever,
practice silent fear.*

*Never must we wail in terror
over disembodied voice of stranger
begging entrance, rattling doorknob,
pounding rifle butt or shoulder into barrier,
hurling curses in frustration,
banned from easy access
to our hiding places.*

*Bullets can penetrate walls and doors
en route toward flesh and bones.
Since crying calls attention
to a body's whereabouts,
practice is required,
how to manage panic.*

*As "lockdown, lockdown"
intercom alarms, training tells us
what to do, and when. Nothing
mitigates against anxiety
caused by either actual assault,
or refresher simulation.*

*Until police and school officials
eventually unlock our classroom door,
fear rises instant, palpable, traumatic,*

continuous, persistent.
Mistrust, distress are loaded,
locked into unsuspicious students
with impressionable hearts.
Dreadfully drilled.

SANDRA: It's terrible that we are forced to plan ahead for gun attacks. Children have to learn to fear for their lives in school? How to protect themselves? That's just not right. We have too many guns. It's not 1950s TV cowboy culture, which was pure fiction even then. If everybody has guns, how can you pick out the good guys?

TERRY: I agree, Sandra. But the fact is, in this state, many believe in the absolute right to bear arms. This is not the time for this discussion...

BARBARA: As more and more states pass open carry laws, a lot of jobs get more dangerous. Nobody can feel safe anymore, not at college, the movies, or a concert. And what about that Afghan War veteran last July who killed five Dallas officers? Armed and trained Texas cops don't want unrestricted gun ownership, either.

SANDRA: A mass shooting already happened at a school like this, Sandy Hook Elementary. The kid's mother bought an assault rifle legally. He took it, killed her first, then killed 26 more at the school. It's always some mentally-ill loner, exercising his Second Amendment right to own a military-grade rifle for hunting.

LINDA: Government officials won't allot funding for mental health services for children or adults. We school nurses have to beg for supplies. Meanwhile the only action politicians want to take is turning schools into prisons with locked doors, checkpoints, armed guards, and school staff forced to be human shields with weapons we aren't qualified to use.

JASON: I feel strongly about our right to feel safe and protected in a school building. Our children must have the same right. My work is designing buildings, with more than one exit for fire safety. Active shooter drills, do they help or do more damage? Children are supposed to feel prepared and therefore safer. But a lot of them get traumatized even when it's only a drill. Adults too.

TERRY: Listen, folks, on this campus, we do have entry restrictions, background checks, and random drills. We're doing the best we can to help everyone feel safer. Please, let's return our focus to the positive effects of mentoring. We came together here today to plan enjoyable things to do with our students this year, remember? Let's continue with the Orientation.

Scene 2

Meeting continues with more explanations, Principal's speech. Veteran mentors tell anecdotes.

Principal Pearl Houston, Ph.D. enters and joins Terry at the front of the room, stage right. Terry nods to acknowledge her presence, but continues her prepared speech.

TERRY: In that packet Carlos gave you, please find the other form that asks for contact data. On it, you'll let me know your available days and times to mentor. I'd also like to know your mentee preferences, grade level, gender, that sort of thing, to help me match you.

Joey Green, a prospective new mentor, raises her hand. Terry calls on her.

JOEY: I've got a question. How do you pick students for us?

TERRY: Various ways. I get teacher referrals. Kids may need extra help with schoolwork or with socialization, for example, if they are shy. Parents sometimes request mentors if several of their kids come here and only one has a mentor. I'll pair Spanish-dominant kids with those of you who are fluent. So many kids need mentors, and we always need bilingual ones. Please let me know any languages besides Spanish you might speak as well. Our students come from a few different countries.

Dr. Houston interjects into Terry's speech.
PEARL: I'm Pearl Houston. As Principal, I sometimes request a mentor for a particular student, if they've been sent to my office too often.
TERRY: Thank you, Dr. Houston. Please tell us more about our school. I'll continue with my speech after you finish.

Terry steps back as Pearl continues.
PEARL: Good morning, everyone. Welcome to Confianza Academy. I've been Principal here for four years, entering my fifth. We've had this mentoring program for many years *(She nods at Sandra, who takes a little bow.)* thanks to Mrs. Kenney. She's helped us recruit many of you repeat mentors. I'm delighted to welcome you all. Thank you for being willing to donate your time.

Confianza serves students from K through 8th grade. We are bilingual and many of our students come here from Spanish-dominant households. Mexican-American families have lived in this neighborhood for generations, all the way back to when Texas was still part of Mexico.

In early grades, Spanish-speaking children are learning English. Starting in grade 4, we expect them to complete class assignments in English. Similarly, teachers also introduce

Spanish to English-speaking students. Everyone is encouraged to use both languages, regardless of which one they learned first. We believe that bilingual fluency is essential. Our children will need to compete for jobs in a global marketplace. Don't worry, we don't require volunteers to be bilingual, but we do value those who are.

Jason interrupts with a question.

JASON: I've read that city public schools have a high percentage of dropouts. Is that because many children get overwhelmed by all that is expected of them?

PEARL: *(annoyed at interruption but civil)* Absenteeism and high dropout rates have complicated causes. Let's not fault the children. Though Confianza's official numbers have been troubling, we have put incentives in place to counter many of the obstacles faced by our students. This mentoring program is just one of these initiatives.

Our neighborhood is less affluent than many. Poverty generates social problems. Our returning mentors have met and helped students who are struggling. Will you veterans please give us some examples?

SANDRA: *(Sandra stands.)* I'm Sandra Kenney. Mentees sometimes are forced by circumstances to change schools. One of my mentees from years ago lived in a large household with many children. She was forced to leave this school after her mother got laid off. They needed a place with cheaper rent.

BARBARA: *(from her seat)* Early on, I mentored a boy whose parents both worked minimum-wage jobs. But they barely made enough to support the family. His older brother had to drop out to go to work, too. My mentee had to spend time on childcare, and had lots of chores around the house, on top of doing his homework.

LINDA: *(Linda stands.)* Hello everyone, I'm Linda Hale. My current mentee, Beryl Fuentes is going into fourth grade. She lives with her mother, aunt, and older brother Tomas. Their home life is unstable. Her mother is very ill. She receives treatments that are debilitating. Her father left them. Her aunt lives there to support her sister in raising the two children. They speak Spanish at home, so Beryl cannot get help with English homework. This year, for the first time, Beryl will need to complete all her assignments in English. I'm happy to help her when she needs it.

CARLOS: Beryl's brother Tomas is my mentee. I'm Carlos Castillo. Tomas is starting sixth grade. His assignments will also be more difficult, this year, especially math. I'm sure Tomas won't have much time to help Beryl with her homework, when he has his own. I hope I can start mentoring soon, to help Tomas keep his grades high, in spite of the turmoil caused by his father's absence.

PEARL: Thank you, mentors. These students from transient home situations, that we call "at-risk," often fall behind in schoolwork and fail to thrive.

JASON: I see. You are faced with economic conditions beyond your control. Standardized test scores don't account for that.

PEARL: That's correct. Our students who are mentored have improved behavior, attendance, and test results. We are able to observe and measure these improvements in other ways besides high-stakes testing. But that doesn't make news like public school failures do.

Pearl's address is interrupted by the Dreamscape, "If Walls Could Talk." Poet Dreamer appears on an elevated platform behind the scrim located at far right behind the main stage. She reads the poem while images of mentors and their students are projected on the other three darkened scrims. The Orientation attendees mime continuing to meet during the Dreamscape.

If Walls Could Talk

In the public school
where this old lady, English speaker,
volunteers to mentor, walls
speak Spanish too.
Las paredes también hablan en español.
Hallways teach geography
by displaying flags of
Spanish-speaking countries
with facts in both their languages.
For example, Argentina's *lesson*
features local favorite
superstar of basketball
who was born there,
Los Spurs' Manu Ginobili.

My new mentee, a fourth grade little girl
at home speaks Spanish.
She can converse in English,
reads schoolbooks well,
but rarely speaks, not even
answering my harmless question,

"What would you like to do together?"
She won't express a choice.
Somehow she learned "Be seen, not heard,"
familiar lesson drilled into little kids.
My parents stunted me this very way
six decades back. So I've resolved
to keep on asking her to choose,
urging her to say what she decides,
unsettling as that seems to be.

I found a Spanish kid book Los oficios de Elmo.
Cuando Crezca Será Maestro
Elmo's Jobs: When I Grow Up
I Want to Be A Teacher.
I asked her help to understand it.
I told her I feel dumb not knowing
how to read en Español.
Reading its giant flap book pages
I demonstrated everybody stumbles
over words by guessing
what I thought some Spanish meant
and being wrong.
She understood and read so fluently
but was reluctant
to the point of silence
to be requested to explain.

We stopped that struggle on the second page
to take up jigsaw puzzle working.
This game we can enjoy together quietly,

*except for briefest commentary
like asking for a match
to certain colored pieces.*

*If walls could talk,
they would not be monolingual.
They would say they want to be connected
to sheltering homes, sweet homes,
instead of fear-filled* prisiónes.

*Building trust is such a complicated process,
slow and threatening compared to
hiding behind walls.
Why don't we each begin by
decorating barriers with stories,
eventually then may come acceptance.*
¿quién sabe? *Who knows?*

PEARL: New folks, I'm certain you'll find mentoring to be as enjoyable and rewarding as our repeat mentors do. Our children show you so much appreciation when you come every week. Again, thank you all for volunteering. Your presence here assists our staff to make public school education more equitable. Now I'll leave you in the capable hands of Ms. Lake. I look forward to seeing you walking our campus hallways with your mentees very soon.

Everybody applauds quietly as Dr. Houston leaves the cafeteria. Terry steps back to center front.

Scene 3

Meeting continues with more introductions. Veteran mentors explain sharing the room using their *Alien Bunny* story.

TERRY: Thank you, Dr. Houston. And thank you, veteran mentors. Please do chime in with anything you think I'm forgetting.

Getting back to my official welcome speech, in that packet Carlos gave you, I've also included our Mentor Handbook, with our school year calendar and contact data for staff. You'll find detailed answers to questions I don't have time to cover here. Briefly, our mentoring program is structured so that you normally come the same one hour every week, except during holidays and testing periods. You can opt out for personal reasons if you need to, or spend less than an hour.

Carlos stands up, hand raised, and Terry recognizes him.

CARLOS: You should say it's wise to call ahead on your mentoring day, to make sure your kid is here. I've left work before, only to find out Tomas was absent. That was a wasted trip.

TERRY: Carlos, I'm so sorry. Thanks for reminding me. Absences do happen. Everyone, please call the attendance clerk on your day. Her number is listed in the Handbook. She has daily reports by 8:15 AM.

But I do know kids try really hard to be here. They come up to me, "Today's my mentor day. Is she coming?" They want to impress you by working hard. You give them one-on-one attention they can't get at home.

Linda stands up as Terry recognizes her to speak.

LINDA: I've had my mentee Beryl since first grade. We're wonderful friends now after three years. But she took quite a while to get comfortable with me. At first, she and I just talked. Gradually, she opened up about things that were bothering her. She's confused about how to respond to her mother's illness. She also gets upset when her brother picks on her. That's normal. I've seen her become more confident speaking with adults. She even started laughing at my jokes.

TERRY: Thanks Linda. The Handbook gives you suggestions of things to talk about with your mentee. You connect on a social level, talking, or even as a writing project. Linda, would you please introduce yourself?

LINDA: Sure, I'm Linda Hale. I'm a retired school nurse. I'm one of the mentors Sandra invited years ago. I speak Spanish, and can help Beryl understand about her mother's treatments. Beryl likes playing card games, especially the one where you build up monster bodies. And checkers.

TERRY: Even while playing a game like checkers, your mentee learns social skills. They are getting your undivided attention. Remember many of them have siblings, and get lost in the crowd. That's why they learn to act up to get attention.

Carlos, you're also returning this year. Please introduce yourself.

CARLOS: *Bueno.* That's right. I'm Carlos Castillo. I came after seeing your video about needing bilingual mentors. You matched me with Tomas two years ago. We don't usually do things with Beryl. They see each other enough at home. Tomas and I want to have our own time together. Tomas likes sports and plays baseball when he can. His favorite teams are the Texas Rangers and the *Saraperos de Saltillo* in the Mexican League. And of course *Los eSpurs.*

Terry, searching for the prospective mentors, notices one is fidgety, and calls on him.

TERRY: Sir, will you please introduce yourself? You mentioned that you design buildings?

JASON: Yes, ma'am. I'm Jason Peterson. I work downtown at an architectural firm. I make technical drawings. That is a practical application of math and science that I'd enjoy sharing with a student. I've been looking for a way to do that. I saw your recruitment PSA so I've come to see what your program offers in terms of organization. Unfortunately, I have to be rigid about how much time I commit here. An older child who's starting to think about careers could be a good match for me. Do you have one who sees himself going to college?

TERRY: Welcome, Jason. Interesting that you mention college. Many children here don't even think about college. Adults in their lives may only have gone to grammar school.

You mentors can be someone they know who has graduated high school and gone to college. You show them it's possible. That said, I can think of an upper grade student who could be a match for you. The girl I'm thinking of excels at math, is interested in robotics, and makes robots.

JASON: *(taken aback but intrigued)* Oh, uh, I hadn't considered ... I suppose a girl would be fine, if she's sharp. Thank you, ma'am.

Terry turns to another new face.

TERRY: Ma'am, you're new. Please introduce yourself. Why did you decide to try mentoring?

JOEY: Sure, I'll go. Hello, everybody. My name is Joey Green. I'm a technician working at a Medical Center clinic. It's Ophthalmology, if you know what that is. Eye doctor. The work I do is fairly routine and repetitive. Same sh..-stuff, different day. I thought I'd try mentoring to spice up my life — in a positive way. Do different things with a kid, creative things. My sister and her husband just had a little girl, so I thought I'd practice before my niece gets old enough to want to play with me. My sister knew about this program. So here I am.

TERRY: Welcome. What are your interests, Joey?

JOEY: Music. I go clubbing on weekends to hear live music when friends are playing. I used to play bass, but don't have much time for that anymore. I could mentor a kid who's interested in music. I also play golf.

SANDRA: What about miniature golf, Joey? Some of us have taken mentees to play that.

JOEY: Sure, that would be fun if it worked out with my schedule.

TERRY: Sandra, you're talking about our field trip. That's a group activity we sometimes organize at the end of the school year. Let's not discuss that until a later meeting. But you'll find group activities explained in the Handbook.

(Resuming her scripted talk) It is wonderful when we have lots of mentors. When two of you need to come at the same exact hour, I can always find a second space, the library, computer lab, my office even. But sometimes it's fun if you all want to play together, maybe a board game, or everybody's favorite, Bingo.

Barbara, you and Sandra arranged to share the room a couple of years ago, right? I remember you all wrote a book together. Please introduce yourselves and tell us about that.

Barbara rises in her spot to speak.
BARBARA: Yes, Sandra and I met with our girls at the same hour. The book we wrote was called *Alien Bunny*.

Let me introduce myself. I'm Barbara Minton, and I've been mentoring here for 6 years. I work in book publishing, so I try to steer my mentees into writing and making their own books. My first mentee was a second grader Angela, one of the *Alien Bunny* authors.

Sandra, will you explain how we wrote *Alien Bunny*?

Sandra stands in her place.
SANDRA: Sure, but let me introduce myself first. Morning, everyone. I'm Sandra, the Mrs. Kenney Principal

Houston mentioned just now. I helped start the program here 9 years ago. I also mentored at another school where I was a special needs teacher. Now I'm retired, but I help Terry recruit and retain volunteers here. Many of us are repeat mentors because it gives us such joy to be agents of change for these children.

Julia was my second mentee here. She co-wrote *Alien Bunny* with Barbara's mentee Angela. The girls were both second graders in different classrooms. They easily became friends, so we all met together. One day, we were talking about what we did over the weekend, and decided to write a story about it.

BARBARA: The girls invented the bunny character. We went camping in the woods and got chased by this Alien Bunny. The girls had such vivid imaginations.

SANDRA: I typed out the finished story. To make books, I cut story pieces apart and the girls pasted them on pages of construction paper. They each drew pictures on different pages. The whole thing wound up taking quite a few weeks.

BARBARA: I remember we made two booklets. The girls each got one to keep, and drew covers on their own copy. And we all autographed them, as authors. Such a big deal.

TERRY: And they read the book to me and to the Principal.

BARBARA: *(jokingly)* That was the extent of their promotional tour. I suppose they made the rounds of their relatives at home, too. They got such a boost to their self-esteem, becoming published authors, right?

BARBARA's voice trails off. Angela Fernandez appears

on an elevated platform behind the scrim located center right behind the main stage. She reads this excerpt from "Alien Bunny" while images from the homemade book are projected on the other three darkened scrims. The Orientation attendees mime continuing to meet during this reading.

Alien Bunny

ANGELA: ... The four campers were hungry, so they fixed hot dogs for dinner and ate s'mores for dessert. It had been an exciting, but somewhat scary day.

As everyone was getting ready for bed in the dark, they noticed that a pair of eyes was looking at them through the trees. It was the Alien Bunny! Angela and Julia shone the flashlight on the eyes.

The creature jumped forward. At first they were frightened, but Angela noticed that he had kind eyes that were blue. She and Julia got closer to him, but he was shy. When they tried to pet him, he ran away.

As the campers laid out their sleeping bags in the huge tent, they heard another noise. It was the Alien Bunny again. When they went outside, he handed Angela and Julia two rings. The girls were very happy to receive these presents. Alien Bunny seemed to be trying to tell them something, but they couldn't understand him because he was talking in rabbit language.

As they watched, Alien Bunny did something to the watch that was on his wrist. It was translating what he said into language that everyone could understand. He was asking, "Will you tell me a story?"

"Well, one day, Angela, Julia and their new friends, Barbara and Sandra decided to go camping in the woods along the San Antonio River..."

Scene 4

Meeting continues, interrupted by a signal bell and class change commotion. Then meeting is halted by an AMBER Alert.

TERRY: Thanks, ladies. I mentioned Bingo a minute ago. Every mentee loves to play that. Bingo is a terrific way for them to learn how to play fair, be a gracious winner and not a sore loser or cheater. The younger ones practice reading numbers and letters. Older students use cognitive skills to figure out how to win, vertically, horizontally, diagonally, or corners....

A loud bell rings throughout the school. This signals class change at 9:20 A.M. for the upper grades. Students pass by noisily outside the permanently open Cafeteria doors. The meeting temporarily stops.

TERRY: *(yelling over din)* Oops. That's the class change bell for the middle grade students. I'm sorry, I should have warned you this would happen. Let's pause for a bit. It's a good time to fill out your forms. Or go ahead and talk among yourselves.

JASON: Or check your emails.

(Class change hallway noise continues. The new people focus on filling out their forms. Barbara and Linda chat privately.)

BARBARA: Linda, do you think you'll have Beryl again this year? My Juan will be back. Terry said he returned his permission slip for this school year already signed. That kid is always so down to earth and efficient. I wonder if, over the summer, he learned chess well enough to beat me.

LINDA: I hope to see Beryl again. I'm prepared to start with a different mentee, though, if she has to leave. Her living situation is so dicey with the dad gone, and her mother getting treatments. Fingers crossed.

We did manage to meet once over the summer. We went to the Zoo with Tomas and Carlos, just after school ended. What a trip! We had to indulge Tomas' short attention span. Eventually we had to split up. The boys only wanted to see stuff we had no interest in, snakes and spiders.

BARBARA: I hope Terry doesn't take more than a week or two to get everybody's paperwork straightened out so we can all start meeting our mentees again.

Barbara's conversation with Linda and the hallway commotion are both interrupted by the Dreamscape, "Hippo Face Off." Poeta También appears on an elevated platform behind the scrim located center left behind the main stage. She reads the poem while images of hippos at the zoo are projected on the other three darkened scrims. The Orientation attendees mime continuing to converse and fill out forms during the Dreamscape.

Hippo Face Off

Hard to believe a hippo could hide, 'tis true.
But their hippos were hidden at the city zoo
in a building full of fish.
Granting his field trip wish
my eager 4th grade friend eventually
found the place,
pool home to three hippos
swimming below surface.
Completely underwater is where
they seem to want to stay.
They raise half a giant heavy head
sometimes in play
above the waterline.
Through tank glass borderline,
one turned her massive bulk around.
Impaired, she trotted at window
through water, stared.
Her head, wide as my
spreadeagled arms sideways
her giant face, with mostly mouth,
did me amaze.

I became alarmed and scared,
but my companion little guy
was unperturbed, undaunted, done.

Sandra, always promoting mentoring at the school, strikes up a conversation with Jason as the hallway commotion continues but gradually subsides.

SANDRA: Jason, what do you think so far? Can you see yourself mentoring here?

JASON: I'm not sure yet. I think your hearts are in the right place. Like you, I also want to do something to help disadvantaged children. Something more tangible than just writing a check. But I've also looked into another program. It expects a one-year commitment, and runs several training sessions before matching you to a child. It's been in business a long time. I find that kind of formally-organized program to be more appealing. I'm torn, though, because I don't think I can commit the amount of time they require.

SANDRA: Please read our Handbook before you decide. We've evolved our methods during nine years of mentoring here. You'll find that the Handbook covers similar questions to the ones in their training sessions. You would spend an hour a week with a child in either program. It's true that we have a more improvised way of approaching mentoring here. But that doesn't make it less effective.

JASON: As I said, my goal is to help an older child take the right steps to prepare for college. Mentoring here seems to be a matter of just-do-it, with not a lot of prep time. I'm not entirely comfortable with that sort of "corporate culture." But with my time constraints, it might work for me. I'd have to live outside of my comfort zone for a couple of hours a week. Growth for me as well as for my student, I suppose. I am thinking seriously about it.

As the chaos from the class change subsides, Terry, who has been chatting with mentors, steps back to center front.

TERRY: OK, Well, that's over with. It just shows how flexible you'll need to be. Never a dull moment here. I'll collect those forms now if you've finished them. Does anyone have questions about items in your packet?

Terry recognizes Joey.

JOEY: How will we be notified when you've chosen the student for us? And how long until we have our first meeting?

TERRY: Believe me, we're all eager to get mentoring started this year. It takes about two weeks to get background check approvals for everybody. Meanwhile, I'll be matching and scheduling you with your students. I'll send you each an email with a short description of your match and a proposed hour to meet. If that's OK with you, we should all be able to start in late September. You can meet your student then.

In the meantime, you've got our Handbook, please read through it. Especially you newbies will find articles about mentoring and activities you might try.

CARLOS: What about those of us who are continuing with our mentees from last year, Terry? Can we come at the same time as last year and start meeting sooner?

TERRY: Carlos, I understand you're eager to start. Problem is, your mentees have advanced a grade and have new schedules. I have to make sure Tomas and the others won't be missing important classwork when they're excused. I will check on that ASAP, I promise.

Smart phones start jangling all over the room as an AMBER

Alert comes through on first one phone, then others. One with a robotic voice breaks through the noise of various phones.

PHONE VOICE: Emergency Alert. Child abduction in San Antonio, TX. Black 2011 Ford F150 XL Pickup with KXPN 4245. Victim is a 15-year-old Hispanic/male, Tomas Fuentes, who was last seen wearing a gray hoodie, blue shirt, tan slacks, and green sneakers. Suspect is a Hispanic/male who is a non-custodial parent, and abducted Fuentes at a school bus stop. Call 9-1-1 with information. Type: AMBER Alert.

Gradually all AMBER Alert alarms go silent. Carlos is upset to hear his mentee's name in the alert. Talking to himself in Spanish, he immediately goes to a corner of the room, speed dials the attendance clerk. He asks about both Fuentes children. Terry collects the pile of returned forms on the table and from folks handing them to her.

LINDA: Terry, is this our Tomas Fuentes? I just assumed he was here today. Beryl, too. I was hoping to peek into her new classroom on my way out.

Carlos hangs up, visibly upset, and moves to Terry's side.

CARLOS: *Dios mio.* I just called the attendance clerk. Tomas is absent today, but Beryl is here. He's been kidnapped by his papa? *No lo creo.* Last June at the Zoo, Tomas told me how excited he was that his papa was coming to visit soon.

Terry, also disturbed by the shock of hearing this about one of the students, rudely shhh's Carlos.

TERRY: Shhh, Carlos, please keep details private. I understand you're upset. This is disturbing.

Terry fights to get back her composure in order to address the others.

Folks, we were just about done. Let's adjourn. If anyone has not completed your forms, please take them with you and email or text a photo back to me ASAP. My number is listed in the Handbook. I'll be back in touch later.

Mentors file out, talking among themselves. Joey had started Googling "AMBER Alert" when her phone stopped sounding.

JOEY: I never really paid that much attention to these alerts. They never directly affected me before. *(holds up her cell phone)* This says a good number of the offenders get caught in the first 3 to 6 hours, especially the ones with plate numbers. If that's any consolation to anybody. I sure hope so. *(She leaves.)*

BARBARA: *(on her way out, to Terry)* Whatever you decide, do it quickly. I've read that abduction cases need to be tracked within the first few hours.

CARLOS: I want to tell the authorities as much as I know about Tomas.

TERRY: Right, Carlos, you probably have insights about him they'll want to know. They probably need to speak with Beryl, too. You said she managed to get here OK, right?

Terry is getting composed again, enough to make choices. She motions to Linda, who is slowly moving to leave.)

Linda, can you stay for a few minutes? Beryl will feel more comfortable with you here. Hopefully she can tell us whatever might have happened at home this morning.

Linda moves back to join Terry and Carlos.

LINDA: Of course, I can stay. I'll do anything to help.

TERRY: I can't believe this is happening. What are we supposed to do next? As a school? I don't know. Let's go see Dr. Houston. We should probably get the school counselor involved, too.

Terry, Linda, and Carlos head for the Principal's office. As they pass the Reception Desk, they see Dr. Houston is already there, greeting and conversing with law enforcement officials. They join that group to say what they know, and be there when Beryl is questioned, to help put a rescue plan in motion.

Scene 5

Same semester, early November. Mentoring has been going on since late September. Two mentors cross paths at the change of the hour.

Linda has just returned to the Mentor Room after having walked Beryl back to class. She is cleaning up craft supplies and a boxed puzzle quickly and putting them back on a shelf. Barbara arrives, stashing her purse before going to pick up her mentee Juan for their weekly visit.

LINDA: Morning, Barbara. Sorry, I'll be out of here in a second. Beryl and I lost track of time.

BARBARA: Oh, no problem. But, since you're here, did you ever hear anything from Beryl about what happened to her brother? I never saw anything in the news about it.

LINDA: Yes. Beryl told me Tomas is fine. He now lives in Saltillo, Mexico with his papa's family. We looked it up and found out it's in Coahuila. It's a big city, like here, with beautiful Spanish colonial architecture from the 1500s. And much older indigenous cultural sites, too. We were both very surprised to find out that Saltillo was the capital of Texas when it was still part of Mexico. You've heard of Saltillo tiles

— they're world famous. We both think it's a good move for Tomas. Beryl misses him, of course, but she's also happy to have more space to herself.

Linda marks her volunteer time in a notebook. Terry comes into the Mentor Room on the way back to her office which is adjacent. She is carrying a pile of mail after having picked it up at the front desk.

TERRY: Morning, ladies.

BARBARA: Hello Terry.

LINDA: Oh, hi Terry, I was just leaving.

TERRY: I heard you talking. Back in September, the same day as that alert, the cops stopped the dad's truck close to the Mexican border. Both parents had a moderated discussion. Mrs. Fuentes finally agreed that Tomas would be better off with his father's people in Saltillo. She accepted how difficult it was for her to care for even one child given her illness. She withdrew the abduction complaint, and allowed Tomas to move.

BARBARA: Thank goodness. That's a relief to hear a happy ending.

TERRY: The one sad thing is, Carlos stopped mentoring. He was deeply affected by suddenly losing Tomas. They had developed a strong bond.

LINDA: Oh, that's why I haven't seen Carlos around. Doesn't he know Tomas is doing well?

TERRY: Yes, I told him. And I encouraged him to come back. We really need our bilingual mentors. I don't think he's ready, though. I guess he's still grieving.

But I'm also going to lose another mentor. Remember

Jason Peterson? He withdrew. He can't continue after the winter break, because he got too busy at work. It's too bad, his seventh grader, Amalia Tamez, was doing really well with him. I need someone for her, hopefully someone with a science background. If either of you might do it, or knows someone to recruit...

BARBARA: OK, I hear you. But right now, let me go get Juan. We're already cutting into his time.

Barbara leaves.

LINDA: Listen, Terry, I've been thinking about getting a second mentee. Beryl's home situation was so unstable. After her brother moved to Saltillo, I wondered if she'd be taken away, too. For now, that seems to be straightened out, but who knows? If you can't find anyone else before the winter break, I'll take on Amalia.

Beryl and I looked up Saltillo, and now she can hardly wait to visit him. We hung drawings she made on the corkboard, see? *(pointing to scrims where these two images are projected)* That's Tomas visiting their dinosaur museum. In the other one he's playing baseball, with a snow-covered peak in the background. Beryl has never seen snow and wants him to show her.

Terry has been sorting through the mail.

TERRY: Thanks Linda, I'm grateful to have that option. I'll definitely show these drawings to Carlos next time I meet with him. See you next week.

As Linda leaves, Terry finds a letter, and says aloud to herself.

Hey, look at this. It's from Tomas, for Carlos. I'm calling him right now.

Terry dials Carlos using her cell phone.

Carlos picks up his cell phone to answer the ring. He is at his desk in a workspace at a research center, which appears on an elevated platform behind the farthest leftmost scrim behind the stage. A bank of computer screens and other research features are projected on the other darkened scrims.

CARLOS: *(a work phone greeting)* This is Carlos Castillo.

TERRY: Hello Carlos. This is Terry Lake from Confianza. I haven't heard from you in a while, how are you?

CARLOS: *Estoy bien, gracias.* I've been busy here at work. It has been a while.

TERRY: I was just speaking with Linda Hale about Beryl. They posted some of her drawings of Tomas in the Mentor Room. I'm letting you know in case you'd like to see them.

CARLOS: *Qué interesante.* Has Beryl heard from her brother recently?

TERRY: I don't know, to be honest. But you have heard from him. I found a surprise in today's mail. Tomas sent you a letter, in care of me. So that's the real reason I called.

CARLOS: *¿Qué? Me escribió* He wrote me? *¡Vaya!* I'm tied up in meetings at work all day today. I will arrange to come tomorrow morning. But please, open it now and read it to me. I have to admit, not knowing how Tomas was doing in Mexico upset me quite a bit.

TERRY: *(She switches to speaker phone, opens the letter,*

and reads slowly.) Okay. Let me put you on speaker. Let's hear what he says. It starts out in Spanish,

> *"¡Hola! Carlos*
> *¡Feliz Día de Acción de Gracias!"*

and a couple more sentences I'll have to leave for you. Then he switches:

> *"I am trying to practice using English here. I hope I won't forget too many words...."*

Terry's voice is replaced with Tomas, who appears on the platform center right behind that scrim. Tomas is in his bedroom in Saltillo, Mexico composing and reading his letter aloud.

As Terry stops reading, an image of the letter is also projected on the center left scrim between Tomas and Carlos. An English translation of the Spanish section is projected on the fourth scrim, the one located at the far right:

[Hello Carlos, Happy Thanksgiving Day. ... As the month of November arises, I become filled with thoughts about family traditions. I am well cared for here by my father and our relatives in Saltillo. I pray daily for my mother's health to improve. May mother, aunt Lupe, and sister Beryl all enjoy happiness during this holiday season. I notice the difference here to have Spanish language spoken by everyone. ... Sincerely, your friend, Tomas.]

> TOMAS: *"¡Hola! Carlos*
> *¡Feliz Día de Acción de Gracias! Comenzo el mes de noviembre. Estoy pensando mucho en las tradiciones familiares. Aqui, en Saltillo, mi padre y mis parientes me tratan muy bien. Cada dia rezo porque mejore la*

salud de mi madre. Ojala que mi mama, tia Lupe y mi hermana Beryl gozen de felicidad durante estas fiestas. Noto la diferencia que hace que todos hablen en castellano aqui.

I am trying to practice using English here. I hope I won't forget too many words. We will be having turkey enchiladas with green mole when we gather together for our family meal.

Carlos, I want to tell you this. Your friendship is one of the blessings of my life in San Antonio, for which I thank God.

It makes me sad that I cannot spend time with you every week like before. You taught me so much and inspired me to think about attending university.

Papa's family is connected with *Instituto Tecnológico de Saltillo* here. I am working hard in the hope to follow your example. Maybe someday I will work at the Research Institute with you.

Thank you for being my mentor and encouraging me during a time when I needed friendship and guidance the most.

Atentamente, su amigo Tomas."

TERRY: Wow, that's amazing. How special.

CARLOS: *(touched) No sé qué decir. ¡Me siento tan abrumado!* I'm so overwhelmed, I don't know what to say. Is there a return address so I can send something back to him? I'll definitely come by tomorrow morning.

TERRY: Yes, he has his address. Congratulations. How

wonderful to hear from Tomas himself what your friendship has meant to him. *(pause)*

I was wondering if this is a good time to ask. Are you ready to consider mentoring again? One of the students is losing her current mentor. Do you remember Jason Peterson?

CARLOS: He was an architect?

TERRY: Yes. He informed me that he needs to withdraw for work reasons.

CARLOS: Let me think about it. When Tomas vanished out of my life, it was such a shock. I didn't feel ready to start with a different mentee. I've been too upset. But I do understand how much you need bilingual mentors. And if I remember correctly, you matched him with this girl because of her interest in robotics.

TERRY: Yes, it is Amalia Tamez. I hope I can find someone, so she won't have to go without a mentor mid-year. I was also very sorry that you lost Tomas so abruptly last fall. These losses are painful for both parties, so disappointing even when the reason is understandable. That's why I think the two of you would be well matched, good for each other. Doesn't the place you work have a division with robotics?

CARLOS: Yes. That's right, I know some people there. If I'm not ready to mentor her myself yet, I will ask around. I'll let you know tomorrow. *(pause)*

Isn't it amazing how Tomas just suddenly reappeared, with gratitude and encouragement? It does make you wonder who mentors who.

TERRY: Yes, and just in time for Thanksgiving. It reminds me of the William Wordsworth poem, where he said, "the Child is father of the Man." Should I expect you first thing tomorrow? I'm here by 7:45 A.M. If I'm out of my office, the front desk can page me.

CARLOS: *Bueno.* Yes. I'll see you then. Maybe you can introduce me to Amalia? *Gracias.*

Terry hangs up, thinking that Carlos may consider mentoring another child.

END OF PLAY

During the first, individual curtain calls, Poet Dreamer appears on the elevated platform behind the scrim located at far right behind the main stage. She reads the poem "Missing Piece (For Jason)" while the other scrims stay dark for the curtain calls. Poet Dreamer joins the rest of the cast onstage after finishing this reading for the last group curtain call.

Missing Piece (For Jason)

I mentor a schoolboy who loves puzzles
but shies away from 4th grade reads.
Our jigsaw games, it's true,
they're fun but I'm more fond
of reading one-on-one.
I noticed he's a kid who imitates
so I'm attempting to inspire him.
One day his teacher sent an article along
for us to read outside of class.
I listened to him struggle,
read aloud while I read
upside down and silently
until he stumbled over words
like "conflict," "diamonds,"
"brutal" work
in tale of children mining gemstones
deep in Congo.
At age of 12, boys graduate
to working physically

*instead of paying teachers cash
to finish school.
They have a choice, if you can call it that,
to mine blood gems and skip
the reading class.
I reminded him he's also 12,
but he objected, stated he's 11 yet
'til next week's celebration.
I see. He always balks
when task is hard.
He finds it wrong to lose.
He must be Number One.
So we turn to different kinds of puzzlement
finding United State shapes
on a jigsaw map.
Texas is the shape he knows
extremely well
with border limits he can easily identify.
I best him 'cuz I hail
from north New Jersey,
old enough to drive through
lots of other states.
May he grow wise enough
to follow roadmaps
puzzling past the borders set before him,
smart enough to understand
the shifting shape of knowledge:
reading is the missing piece
he needs to always win.*

2

Introduction to the Poems

I wrote a whole series of poems about my relationships with mentees for a dozen years between 2009 and 2021. More recently, proliferation of Covid-19 viruses eliminated volunteer visits to public schools. Also, mass shootings have jeopardized volunteers' comfort with on-site mentoring, particularly in Texas schools.

Only three of my original mentoring poems — "If Walls Could Talk," "Hippo Face Off," and "Missing Piece (For Jason)" — survived the editing process to remain as Dreamscapes in the Mentor Wonders script.

The fourth included poem — "Locked, Loaded, Dreadfully Drilled" — emanated from my reflection about the Uvalde, Texas, elementary school shooting that occurred during script development. Facts in that case negate all the excuses lawmakers use to justify accepting campaign donations from gun advocates to serve their interests instead of prioritizing the mental health and safety of school children.

A few of these poems have been published in various anthologies, which I've acknowledged. A portion of "If Walls Could Talk" even won a contest to be published as a VIA bus poster during National Poetry Month in April 2019.

But a collected volume has not appeared until now. By reproducing them here within my self-published Mentor Wonders manuscript, I hope to give future presenters of the drama an option to include more of these lyrical anecdotes in a theatrically creative way.

I have gathered poems about being a mentor and a couple where I was mentored, including:

- Locked, Loaded, Dreadfully Drilled
- If Walls Could Talk
- Hippo Face Off
- Missing Piece (For Jason)
- Age Difference
- Messy Business
- Laces Rule
- Cake Mix Stories
- Cobalt: Keeping What Passed Present
- 'Rithmetic: Fractions, Mysteries, Curiosities
- Like Dominos
- Crescendo
- When This Mentor Gets Puzzled
- Keeping Score
- Acknowledgments

Age Difference

She says I'm older than her grandpa
(causing aging fears)
I guess she's younger than my dog
(in human years)
She hears "Who made this
playroom mess" complaints
Admits her sloppy playtime,
mixing brightly colored paints.
My mentee loves such art activity,
I must admit
But I can't allow custodian
to throw a hissy fit.

Messy Business

My mentee is a youthful beauty
with a contagious, ready smile.
In a different home
she could be a fashion model
leveraged by parental privilege
into opportunity and wealth
headed easily toward a star's career.
In her home, she and all her
siblings help crack *huevos*
so carefully, to save the eggshells
daily, almost a prayerful practice.
They color them,
and fill them with confetti
making *cascarones*
for mom to market at Fiesta
a dozen for a dollar,
to maybe earn some extra cash.

I'm her mentor at the school. Or is she mine?
I say I never knew confetti eggs existed
until I moved to Texas from the frigid North.

I have one dozen, never played with
since my friends don't care for
combing little papers from their hair,
cleaning up the mess.

This makes her laugh,
and flash her drop-dead gorgeous smile.
She makes me want to use my privilege,
buy a dozen dozen dozen from her mother,
so all of us can play a hybrid game,
South Texas style, eggs thrown like
in a snowball fight,
learn how to deal with mess.

It's a child, not a budget choice.
It's a mind, not a dollar sign.
Why can't we make great, safe, free
public schools our bottom line?

Laces Rule

Though I have never actually observed a youngster
trip on untied laces, I issue just this warning to
my mentored hallway-racing 3rd grade boys.
Does their unkempt footwear
showcase carelessness?
As in, they could not care less
about their shoes' appearance?
It's obvious they do competitively care
who wins the sprint.
I observe so many knots in one kid's laces
he could never hope to tie them neatly into bows.
I need another strategy, if I want to stimulate
their interest in tidy shoes.
I found online about 4 dozen choices
how to lace a sneaker.
These lacing methods, some with doubled colors,
do require math skills we can learn,
like counting keyholes, brads,
and calculating lace length to fit shoe size.
Young athletes seeking footwear
to enhance their race performance

could learn to modify the speed
and comfort of their stride,
with shoelace engineering.
Next visit, I propose we try to make
enticing loops of shoelace art.
Would anybody toss these guys' artistic sneakers
up and over wires near their school?
Maybe they could have the latest thing
in schoolyard admiration:
untied laces get transformed
to sneakers looking fly
when flashy laces rule.

Cake Mix Stories

When I arrived to mentor, my second grader's class
was working their assignment:
make up a story; tell us how to do something
writing in full sentences.
I was asked to help her finish that.
Sounds fun, I told her, I do it all the time.
She loves working jigsaw puzzles, playing games,
schoolwork not so much.
She is good at reading, and is picking up
the way to spell an unknown word
by sounding out the syllables.
But now she couldn't think of anything to say.
I prompt with questions, asking
what she does at home with mama.
"Make a chocolate cake." Yum.
Tell me what you do. Write that down.
"Mix ingredients, put it in the oven.
Take it out and eat it."
Her every answer is a word or two,
commands and cake ingredients.
I remind her she's supposed to write

full sentences, tell me how.
Obedient, her pencil traces words,
then "How do you spell 'oven'?"
A word that does not lend itself
to sound-it-out.
My questions underscore an elder's baker biases.
What kind of chocolate? Chips or bars to melt?
"It's in the cake mix." Oh, okay.
What should you do with cake mix?
"Break eggs into the cake mix."
How many eggs? Are they cold?
"Two eggs." Any other liquid? Water, milk?
An abundance of erasing and rewriting
happens on her paper in her determination
to create full sentences.
Yet all this tedious printing happens
while half-open puzzle box and Topple game
are teasing her with better things to do.
I dislike denying her that fun
but teacher asked my help so
she could finish work.
It seems to me that she has trouble
seeing details in her mind. Could acting help?
I suggest that we pretend the puzzle box is mix,
Topple tree is mixer, its box the pan,
and another student desk nearby an oven.
Write this down, how do you get the batter
from this mixer here to pan
and that into the oven there?
She writes that sentence. Done.

Does she think her story's good enough
to make the highest grade?
Fine, we move along to Topple.
I say, just sayin'
you could also write a different story.
What if this mentor room is a magic kitchen?
After you mix it, batter pours itself in pan,
pan flies into oven without spilling any,
oven knows how long to bake.
When anybody eats this magic cake,
they too can fly.
My story made her smile.
I hope it grows her wings.

Cobalt: Keeping What Passed Present

Last week my little mentored girlfriend
fashioned bride and groom from clay
she elaborated woman dressed in gown and crown
with juicy big blue lips.
When she, as preacher, made them kiss
the maiden's mouth hilariously stuck to his.
The home she had her groom build for his wife,
of gingerbread-like cardboard frames, was erected,
dressed with paper snow and candy canes,
its façade appearing youthfully adorned,
colorfully embellished like a wedding song.

This week my piano touching buddy texted
from afar by way of self-rebuke "fuck me"
emphatically NOT meaning that ejaculation
quite the way I would have liked to see.
Yet I could drink a case of such an ambiguity!
He did mail long-anticipated plastic discs eventually
enclosed — I hold — those potent

harmonies of mutual perception,
delight recorded of a past still present
in our sound extraction
bedecked with malleable spirit's tone
radiocobalt given lip within this poem.

'Rithmetic: Fractions, Mysteries, Curiosities

Her teacher wants me to work on fractions
with my little girl. "Uh oh," says that part of me
convinced I'm bad at math since flunking Calc
in college. "OK," slowly says
the grown-up's mouth, "I'll try."
How does a woman living well past
one-half her life's potential hundred years;
a few more than three-quarters of 80,
but still a ways away, four-fifths of 90
come to track her aging on a fraction strip?
Visualize, so long is mine, compared to this child's
diminutive one-tenth portion, so differently wise.
Numerator over denominator, what's that mean?
I know but it's a mystery HOW I know,
to answer 4th grade book's command:
"Explain your answer."
"Let's leave that one for your teacher
and move on," I say.
Or should we both explore?

To make these fractions fun instead of hard,
we cut up colored paper into thirds
to craft our handmade votive candle covers
luminarias, she calls them.
We measure with a ruler where to make our cuts.
This activity reveals arrays of tick marks,
different lengths, between the inches numbered.
Which line is the right one? We can count.
Like me, she also figures work-arounds
to keep from handling rulers, measure-tools.
She visualizes problems spatially;
measuring one piece to use to model more.
I hadn't taken notice until this moment that
child-eyes see as total blurs
these calculating mysteries.
A new 'rithmetic task for me:
to cultivate her curiosities.

Like Dominos

I usually intimidate my fourth grade friend
when I ask her to decide about activities
in the mentor room at school.
We have too many choices
what to do. I offer grown up things
I'm fond of: reading books,
making crafts or drawing.
Things I've done with other kids
before, like jigsaw puzzles
— sometimes missing pieces —
board games, building blocks,
or checkers, sometimes played
with chessmen if they think
the royal characters are cool.
Not chess when youngster brains
can hardly grasp the movement rules
for all those medieval personalities.
I wonder when I'm being flexible with rules
to make up other ways to play these
tainted games, am I modeling
an undesirable role?

This day it's dominos she wants to try
when we turn up a box of tiles.
At my advancing age with "CRS"
(I "can't remember stuff")
I vaguely recollected rules I played
with sisters at our grandma's every week.

> We did not score from counting pips.
> Tiles were laid out upside down;
> one upside up began the board;
> took turns, each picking one. You match to
> numbers facing up; if you didn't
> have a match in hand, you picked again
> from "boneyard" — what we called it —
> 'til you matched; first player
> done with all their tiles would win.

We tried that game but soon observed
this tile collection never has been used
for matching numbers. Random tiles
were duplicates and others altogether lost,
Most children, I suppose, had played
that other game, the one of setting vertically
a string of tiles that knock each other down.

While she made topple lines like that,
I sought another set of dominos.
I found a sack with several different colored sets.
"Let's see if we can make a proper set
of black ones we can play."
She agreed; with doubled numbers on both tile halves

we arranged them
>"0" with 1,2,3,4,5,6
>"1" with 2,3,4,5,6
>"2" with 3,4,5,6
>"3" with 4,5,6
>"4" with 5,6
>"5" with 6

in a pleasing pattern visually
that revealed immediately
which tiles were gone irrevocably.
With full black set assembled,
we felt satisfied, investigated other tiles:
red set: missing some;
yellow: full but hard to read white spots;
blue set: missing quite a few.
We grouped these in a multicolored set
for toppling fun, and wrote a warning
note for future players.

One official game of dominos
we played with our black set, then
boxed it up responsibly.
We both enjoyed this graphic puzzle,
improvising how to check the tiles,
identify, correct irregularities.
We figured how to fix annoying glitches
facing other kids and mentors.
Together we made problems fall away
like dominos.

Crescendo

She knew instinctively, it is music is a godsend.
But this little girl was trained
to be unseen, not heard.
She did it well, performed superbly
most of her adult life –
well, some.

Her mother would not finish playing piano,
any tune she started.
Why do you suppose?
Though beg to listen daughter did,
beg for lessons they could not afford.

She knew instinctively, playing keyboard
is physical: finger, ankle, wrist and spine activity,
also exercising brainpan, spirit.
Exertion toward creation.

Though musicians, also poets (some her lovers)
got climaxing all confused inside her mind,

between their skins crescendo registers her loving,
stirring heartstrings.

At such vast distance from smooth moves,
she struggles now.
What gives with these conflicted instincts?
When sounding keys, some welling up
of god connection vibrates
she recalls all loved ones planted seeds
her swelled anatomy still carries
need, ongoing, reach someone who'll help her
come to understand how basic music theory
deeply circles, in lucent propagation.

Tones resound — unfailingly — profound
godsent intelligence
that learns and teaches resonance
with infallibility.

Tentative, her human hands traverse
free will's contrasted
black and white geography
to essay into harmony
that which might not always perfect be.

When This Mentor Gets Puzzled

For ages 10 and up, its four straight
solid yellow borders,
should be simple to assemble, I suppose.
But piecing outer sides together with
my first grader, I'm frustrated
while he places colored middle chunks
of some Transformer robot image
smartly, quickly with triumphant taps and shouts.
If this struggle needs to be a race to finish,
I suppose my young friend wins.

Keeping Score

Scoring 10th grade student essays
assignment was, Explore:
> *when Rolling Stones sang timeless phrase*
> *"You can't always get what you want..."*
> *tell the reader what you wanted,*
> *did not get; how you relate to this, explain.*

Most of these young writers, what they wanted,
out of reach was stuff, consumer products —
    Xbox 360: parents thought too pricy
    new car to celebrate a 16th year and licensed:
    depreciation killed that pretty ride
    puppy, pony, dirt bike, ATV: longing
    trumped by safety fear.
Another hefty group of teens was looking for
    athletic triumph for their team
    or precious spot on drumline, cheering squad:
    learn patience now, perhaps next year.
As these responses reappeared
it seemed test monitors permitted hints,
suggestions on the wall.

These are high-stakes assessments, after all.

We scorers are ourselves compared
for client quality to be assured.
Should same response's double score
be deviant by more than 1,
alarm is raised, retraining is endured
before another piecework item hits your queue.
Compensation by the piece
means scorer's paycheck suffers.
Can't always get what computer-tethered
effort's worth.

A boy I thought deserved the highest score,
a 4 for innovative thought,
related how he intervened between
a bully and his mark.
A fight ensued and he, the dark-skinned one
latecomer viewers decided was aggressor,
made perpetrator trip to principal,
who sent him home, while bully got away
to hunt another day for hapless schoolmate prey.
Justice is what this young, black,
and (in my opinion) gifted writer didn't get.
Vindication. At that time.

And then another scorer
thought his essay only worth an average 2.
I made a spirited defense
of both his ethics and my rubric reading.

Dismayed to say Stones lyric told it true:
when what you want, for no good reason
does not always come to you:
my scoring supervisor
amplified the unjust crime.

But we are keeping score.
Testing system 0
That student earned his 4.

Acknowledgments

"Crescendo"

- Published in *In the Words of Womyn (ITWOW) International 2016 Anthology*/edited by Jenuine Poetess & Sarah Frances Moran. Yellow Chair Press, April 26, 2016, pg 18.
- Also appeared in *Kinda Pregnant* (2013), artist handmade, signed numbered limited edition of 40, np.

"Hippo Face Off"

- Incorporated as a Dreamscape in the poetic drama, Mentor Wonders, a video production of released in November 18, 2022
- Awarded 2nd Place in Alamo Area Poetry Society contest, The Child in You, May 7, 2022
- Published in *ZOOanthology,* Steve Carr, ed., Sweetycat Press, Aug 10, 2022

"If Walls Could Talk"

- Incorporated as a Dreamscape in the poetic drama, Mentor Wonders, a video production of released in November 18, 2022
- Published as a poster for display on VIA Poetry on the Move buses during National Poetry Month, April 2019
- Performed at award ceremony March 28, 2019

"Locked, Loaded, Dreadfully Drilled"

- Incorporated as a Dreamscape in the poetic drama, Mentor Wonders, a video production of released in November 18, 2022

"Messy Business"

- Featured poem at *Wolff Literary Journal,* February 28, 2019 https://wolffpoetry.com/messy-business-poem-by-catherine-lee/
- Appeared in *Kinda Pregnant* (2013), artist hand-made, signed numbered limited edition of 40, np.

"Missing Piece (For Jason)"

- Incorporated as a Dreamscape in the poetic drama, Mentor Wonders, a video production of released in November 18, 2022
- Excerpt published in *The Thing Itself,* (2018) Our Lady

of the Lake University, Issue 45, pp. 76-77 (link no longer works)

Stage with Cafeteria

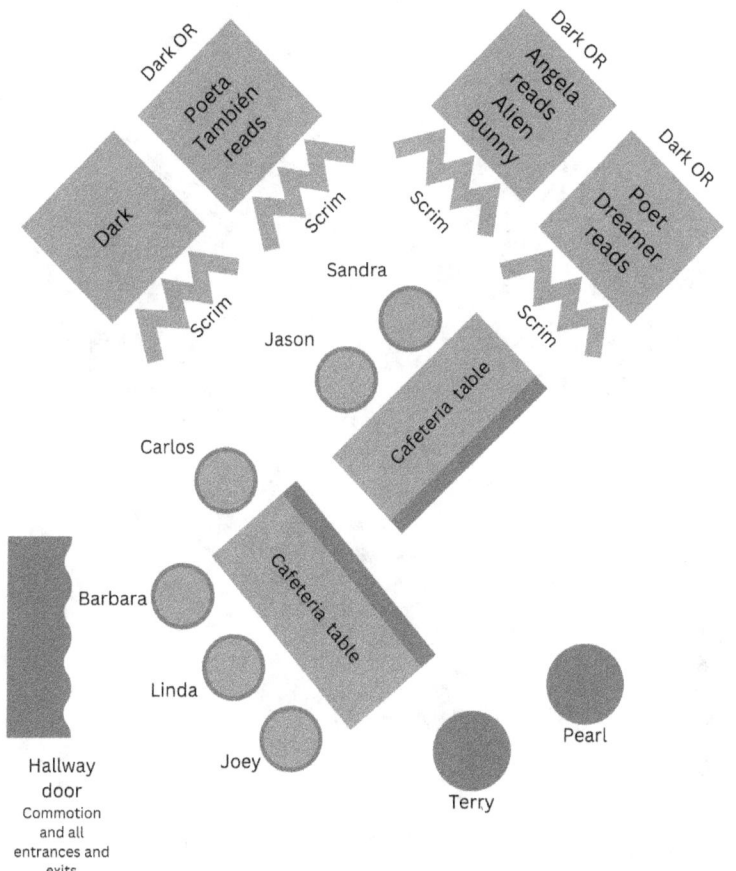

Scenes 1-4 - Cafeteria

Stage with Mentor Room

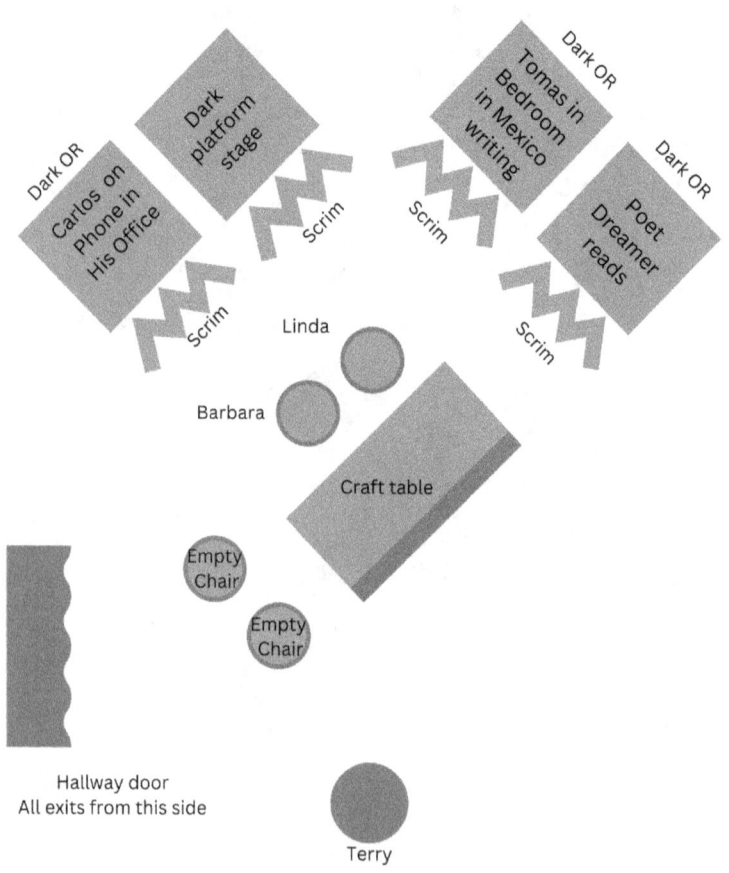

Scene 5 - Mentor Room

Property List

(Use this space to create props list for your production)

Sound Effects

(Use this space to create sound cues lists for your production)

- S1 - Lockdown Alarm
- S4 - Class Change Bell
- S4 - children walking in hallway
- S4 - AMBER Alert voice message
- S4 - AMBER Alert phone alarms

Sound Effects

(Use this space to create sound cues lists for your production)

Notes

(Use this space to make notes for your production)

Notes

(Use this space to make notes for your production)

About The Author

Catherine Lee is a neo-Beat who began exploring poetry as a percussive voice at Studio Red Top, Inc., a loft space, later nonprofit organization she founded in Boston MA in 1978. Her inspiration for creating this salon attempt was her English professor, Percy E. Johnston, who invited her into his New York City loft, Studio Tangerine, in 1970. Until 1995, Lee produced hundreds of concerts, workshops, jam sessions, readings, radio and video broadcasts, and exhibits, including joint performances (1986-87) with her mentor, Beat poet/hipster tedjoans. Ted's "Jazz is my religion" griot legacy continually inspires her.

Late in 2006, Lee relocated to San Antonio TX; she also spent creative time in Asheville NC (summers of 2014-2018). She focuses on writing, seeking publication and performance opportunities, creating altered book editions of chapbooks, and recording her poetry whenever possible. Composer/trumpeter/educator Cecil Reenald Carter, an occasional collaborator, contributed original music to the Dramatic Reading video of this Mentor Wonders script, available on VIMEO.

Lee has performed with senior readers theater companies since 2014. Mentored by actor/director Bill Gundry, Lee presented poetry and dramatic roles in theater recitals at Bihl Haus, The Playhouse Cellar Theater, and various San Antonio libraries and Senior One Stop Centers. In late 2017, noted character actor Tony Plana joined Gundry as producer/co-director of the re-envisioned Seniors In Play (SIP) repertory company. During 2020's Covid-19 lockdown, SIP performances migrated from stage to Zoom small-screen video. Plana became more actively involved as director following Mr.

Gundry's sudden, untimely death in February 2021. With this direction and encouragement, Lee employed new skills to write drama for video delivery. She secured funding from the City of San Antonio Department of Arts & Culture to develop this Mentor Wonders script through a series of recorded online rehearsals.

Lee received a BA in English from Montclair State University NJ. While doing graduate level coursework in Linguistics at University of MA, Amherst, Lee applied transformational grammatical analysis to poetic language. Her writing embodies the thesis she developed that fine poetry uses certain words that pivot, encompassing multiple meanings by holding semantic and/or syntactic ambiguity.

Lee augments income from arts and performances with nonprofit grant writing and other freelance writing through Jazz-Ovation-Inn.com.

www.ingramcontent.com/pod-product-compliance
Lightning Source LLC
Chambersburg PA
CBHW051955290426
44110CB00015B/2250